Austerities

By Charles Simic

AUSTERITIES

Poems by

Charles Simic

GEORGE BRAZILLER

New York

Some of these poems have previously appeared in the following periodicals to whose editors grateful acknowledgment is made: *Antaeus, Quarterly West, The Paris Review, The New Republic, Field, Ploughshares, Poetry Miscellany, The Carolina Quarterly, The New Boston Review, The Partisan Review, Durak, Ironwood, Skyline, kayak, Ethos.*

"February" and "Rural Delivery" were first published by *The New Yorker.*

"Crows" and "Drawn to Perspective" appeared in *The Atlantic Monthly.*

Published in the United States in 1982 by
George Braziller Inc.
Copyright © 1982 by Charles Simic

For information address the publisher:
George Braziller, Inc.
One Park Avenue
New York, N.Y. 10016

Simic, Charles, 1938–
    Austerities: poems.
    (Braziller series of poetry)
    I. Title.
PS3569.I4725A95   811'.54   82–4289
ISBN 0-8076-1043-7   AACR2
ISBN 0-8076-1044-5 (pbk.)

Printed in the United States of America
First Edition

for HELEN

"Of the world, weather-swept, with which
one shares the century."

George Oppen

Contents

I

II

III

I

HISTORY

On a gray evening
Of a gray century,
I ate an apple
While no one was looking.

A small, sour apple
The color of woodfire,
Which I first wiped
On my sleeve.

Then I stretched my legs
As far as they'd go,
Said to myself
Why not close my eyes now

Before the Late
World News and Weather.

SPOONS WITH REALISTIC DEAD FLIES ON THEM

I cause many worries to my mother.
My body will run with the weeds some day.
My head will have its slaughterhouse-ants,
Its carnivorous, bloody-aproned ants.

That was not in your legends, saints!
How she worked as a saleslady in a novelty store:
Joy buzzers and false beards
Between her and immortal life.

A room she rented from a minor demon.
Dog star and a coffee mill for company.
A hand-operated one for each of her guardian angels
To take a turn grinding —

Though I'm not a believer —
Neither is she, and that's why she worries,
Looks both ways at the crossing
At two gusts of nothing and nothing.

AUSTERITIES

From the heel
Of a half loaf
Of black bread,
They made a child's head.

Child, they said,
We've nothing for eyes,
Nothing to spare for ears
And nose.

Just a knife
To make a slit
Where your mouth
Ought to be.

You can grin,
You can eat,
Spit the crumbs
Into our faces.

AN EVENING WITH THE MASTER

With a bird-whistle
He invites my soul in
Makes it perch on his shoulder
Makes it eat out of his hand

The eyes' unfathomable delicacies
For supper
Giddy bones of the inner ear
For midnight snack

With a stick and a leather glove
He teaches it to copy with its claws
The somber treatises
Of Johannes Kepler and Isaac Newton

Diagrams of celestial kennels
Fire-escapes
Burglar-alarms
That protect its father's mansion

A soul with a falcon's hood
Bent over a nursery school slate
Which screeches and bleeds darkly
As it lets itself be written

CROWS

Just so that each stark,
Spiked twig,
May be even more fierce
With significance,

There are these birds
As further harbingers
Of the coming wintry reduction
To sign and enigma:

The absolutely necessary
Way in which they shook snow
Out of their wings,
And then remained, inexplicably

Thus, wings half-open,
Making two large algebraic x's
As if for emphasis,
Or in the mockery of . . .

THE CHILDHOOD OF PARMENIDES

for Elektra Haviaris

For asking, why is there something
Rather than nothing?
The schoolmaster sends the little punk
To see the Principal.

Unfortunately, they haven't got one yet.
There's only King Minos and his labyrinth,
And of course, Philemon, who's about to die
   laughing
At the sight of an ass eating figs.

FEBRUARY

The one who lights the wood stove
Gets up in the dark.

How cold the iron is to the hand
Groping to open the flue,
The hand that will draw back
At the roar of the wind outside.

The wood that no longer smells of the woods;
The wood that smells of rats and mice—
And the matches which are always so loud
In the glacial stillness.

By its flare you'll see her squat;
Gaunt, wide-eyed;
Her lips saying the stark headlines
Going up in flames.

INHERITANCE

This is my father's gray blanket.
He used to lie under it anonymous:
Head and face hidden, bare feet
Sticking out, their toes clenched.

On a windy November afternoon,
The house cold, even
The bright sunlight chilling,
Just as it is now —

Like a steel tape measure
Estimating the anatomy of the sleeper,
The position of the heart
Under this blanket meant for a narrow bed —

An army cot perhaps? O recruits,
Prisoners! I believe one covers one's head
Because the lights are left on
In cells throughout the night.

ROUGH OUTLINE

The famous torturer takes a walk
Whom does he see standing there in the snow
A pretty girl in a wedding dress
What are you doing out there all alone in the cold

You're the famous torturer much feared
I beg you to spare my love
Who is in your darkest prison cell
I wish to marry him etc.

I will not give back your bridegroom
He must be tortured tonight
By me personally
You can come along and help him lament his fate

She remained where she was
The night was cold and very long
Down by the slaughterhouse a dog-like creature howled
Then the snow started to fall again

LATE

No one washes the bloody clothes.
They hang on the line
With their bullet holes
Left intact.

In the gathering dusk,
A mother's voice
Calls her children to supper
Over the roofs of the world.

I think one of the crows
Will have to go instead.
I think the blackest one on the fence
Will have to wear shoes
And climb the back stairs.

FABLE

for Mekeel

In my favorite one,
The fox is nagging
The crow to sing.

It's a dead oak tree
He's sitting in
Surrounded by acres of snow.

The winter evening,
Exceptionally cold,
Long-shadowed, hushed.

We know he closes
His eyes tight
In anticipation.

The fox is long gone
With her toothsome prize.

Ah, the obituary bird!
Singing his heart out, sobbing too—
And it could be worse.

RURAL DELIVERY

I never thought we'd end up
This far north, love.
Cold blue tinge in lieu of heavens.
Quarter moon like chalk on a slate.

This week it's subtraction
And the art of erasure we study.
O the many blanks to ponder
Before the arctic night overtakes us
One more time on this lonely stretch of road
Unplowed since morning,
Snowmittens raised against the sudden
Blinding gust of wind,
But the mailbox empty.
I had to stick my bare hand
All the way to nothing and no one
To make absolutely sure
This is where we live.

The wonder of it! It seemed,
We retraced our footsteps homeward
Lit up by the same fuel as the snow
Glinting in the gloom
Of the early nightfall.

SHAVING AT NIGHT

Like the profile of a man who waits
To be arrested at dawn.
If not this night, well, then
Some other night soon.

The small suitcase already packed,
The family long dispersed,
One sits fully dressed
With the ashtray, the clock, the quiet.

Then, the inexplicable shave:
The face in the slanting mirror
Lit by a dim bulb, one eye shut—
The face one won't look at closely—

Not yet anyway, while
There's still the upper-lip to shave,
The chin, the throat
With its large adam's apple.

II

THE WORK OF SHADING

Rain color of pencil-lead,
Color of old erasers,
The fifth grade teacher's
Asleep at his desk.

The students are studying
The details of graying hair,
The frayed shirt-collar,
But now it has started to rain hard.

Ordinarily one sees in the distance
A stretch of weed-choked marshland
On a far side of which is a city
With a plume of black smoke.

AN ANTIQUATED TUB

Supported by four lions' paws
Into which a swan-necked
Copper faucet drips
Throughout the long night

The grave deliberations
Of phantom courts
And hanging juries
Over the fate of each drop

In the half-light of
The patiently scoured enamel —
Long pauses
In which to plumb

Lengths and depths
To imagine the next drop's
Convolutions
The long-held-out cry of its name —

Sight of its shirt-tails
As it proceeds
Breakneck
Into the swill

HURRICANE SEASON

Just as the world was ending
We fell in love,
Immoderately. I had a pair of

Blue pinstripe trousers
Impeccably pressed
Against misfortune;

You had a pair of silver,
Spiked-heeled shoes,
And a peekaboo blouse.

We looked swank kissing
While reflected in a pawnship window:
Banjos and fiddles around us,

Even a gleaming tuba. I said,
Two phosphorescent minute-hands
Against the Unmeasurables,

Geniuses when it came to
Undressing each other
By slow tantalizing degrees . . .

That happened in a crepuscular hotel
That had seen better days,
Across from some sort of august state
    institution,

Rainblurred
With its couple of fake
Egyptian stone lions.

EAST EUROPEAN COOKING

While Marquis De Sade had himself buggered,
O just around the time the Turks
Were roasting my ancestors on a spit,
Goethe wrote "The Sorrows of Young Werther."

It was chilly, raw, bleak, down-at-the-mouth
We were slurping bean soup with smoked sausage
On 2nd Avenue where years before I saw a horse
Pull a wagon loaded with flophouse mattresses.

Anyway, as I was saying to my friend
Before the waiter brought the fried calf's liver,
It wasn't half as bad then as it is today.
In fact, the sufferings were almost lyrical in
    comparison.

"What the hell are you talking about?" he yelled.
And he had two front teeth missing . . .
Eventually, he calmed down and said:
"I make no distinctions between murderers."

Which brought another bottle of Hungarian wine,
And some dumplings stuffed with prunes.
"I mean, it's not like keeping crickets in a cage . . .
The thing is serious, and it's not over yet . . ."

Luckily, we had this Transylvanian waiter,
This ex-police sergeant, ex-dancing school instructor
Regarding whom we were in complete agreement
Since he didn't forget the toothpicks with the bill.

STRICTLY BUCOLIC

for Mark and Jules

Are these mellifluous sheep,
And these the meadows made twice-melliferous by their
    bleating?
Is that the famous mechanical wind-up shepherd
Who comes with instructions and service manual?

This must be the regulation white fleece
Bleached and starched to perfection,
And we could be posing for our first communion pictures,
Except for the nasty horns.

I am beginning to think this might be
The Angelic Breeders Association's
Millennial Company Picnic (all expenses paid)
With a few large black dogs as special guests.

These dogs serve as ushers and usherettes.
They're always studying the rules,
The exigencies of proper deportment
When they're not reading Theocritus,

Or wagging their tails at the approach of
Theodora. Or is it Theodosius? Or even Theodoric?
They're theomorfic, of course. They theologize.
Theogeny is their favorite. They also love theomachy.

Now they hand out the blue ribbons.
Ah, there's one for eveyone!
Plus the cauldrons of stinking cabbage and boiled turnips
Which don't figure in this idyll.

ROSALIA

I

An especially forlorn human specimen
Answers a marriage-ad
On a street of compulsory misfortune,
One drizzly November afternoon.
Sorrow waiting with her doilies
In a dining room with a spider-legged chandelier
Which the subway rattles from time to time.
A cup of herb tea with a bride's eyelash
Floating in it.
Homemade cakes the size and color of
A little finger caught in the door.
There's also her grandfather's saber on the wall,
And the story of how the Angel of Death
Snatched her purse
On the way home from the evening Mass.

II

She saw the Archangel Michael, too.
(That she told no one.)
She cooked dinner for her blind old mother,
Fed her with a baby spoon.
In a small, shabby office,
She entered figures in a crook's ledger,
Sharpened pencils with a razor blade.
Then she thought of Mr. O'Reilly.
Like a lone customer waiting in a barbershop
On a street of palatial funeral parlors,
A bridegroom with the eyes of someone
Who has been peeling onions,
But that can't be
Since he's in this oldtime barbershop
Empty but for the mirrors.

III

Rosalia and her mother moved away
But no one knows where and why.
They directed me to the Italian bakery.
My cakes, said the baker with the glass eye,
Are like cheeks and dimples on an old fashioned
 china doll.
Next, I stopped at the undertaker's.
We import our pillows and tassels from Arabia.
We also sell postcards of the next life—
And already, I was talking to some tarot-readers,
Madame Olga and Madame Esmeralda in spiked heels
Outside a storefront church on a windy night.
Images of Saints favored by fugitives from justice.
O trombones and tambourines!
White snowflakes falling for Rosalia Rissi
But as many lampblack ones!

PIETY

A plain black cotton dress
On a wire hanger
In a closet otherwise empty,
Its door ajar to the light.

If you open your eyes,
You'll note it sways ever so slightly,
It shudders in the draft
Of undetermined origin.

Or is it your own breath?
Reaching that far
Despite the miles of frozen
Stubble, stone, earth.

If you close your eyes,
There's even a tiny rip
On the level of thighs,
The curlicue of blackest thread.

THUS

Blue devils'
Bluest
Offspring—
My wife.

I said,
Pascal's own
Prize abyssologist
In marriage.

On her knees
Still scrubbing
The marble stairs
Of a Russian countess.

Once long ago in Paris
Gathering the butts
Outside the fashionable cafes
For her unemployed father.

Or in the New World
Naked before the grim
Doctor and nurse
A murmur in the heart.

Nevertheless, poking
The spit-moistened
End of a black thread
At the unblinking needle's eye,

Twelve hours a day.
A sublime seamstress,
An occupation hard on the backbone
And the eyesight.

On dark winter Sundays
Difficult to squint out
The letters and foreign words
In the night school textbook.

All the carefully dog-eared,
Underlined passages
About lynchings, tar-featherings,
Witch-burnings —

Next to a cup of black coffee —
The kind storefront gypsies make
When they sit staring at the rain,
Their lips just barely moving.

MIDPOINT

No sooner had I left A.
Than I started doubting its existence:
Its streets and noisy crowds;
Its famous all-night cafes and prisons.

It was dinnertime. The bakeries were closing:
Their shelves empty and white with flour.
The grocers were lowering their iron-grilles.
A lovely young woman was buying the last casaba melon.

Even the back alley where I was born
Blurs, dims . . . O rooftops!
Armadas of bedsheets and shirts
In the blustery, crimson dusk . . .

*

B. at which I am destined
To arrive by and by
Doesn't exist now. Hurriedly
They're building it for my arrival,

And on that day it will be ready:
Its streets and noisy crowds . . .
Even the schoolhouse where I first
Forged my father's signature . . .

Knowing that on the day
Of my departure
It will vanish forever
Just as A. did.

BIOGRAPHICAL NOTE

A rat came on stage
During the performance
Of the school Christmas play.
Mary let out a scream
And dropped her infant
On Joseph's foot.
The three Magi remained
Frozen
In full regalia.
You could hear a pin drop
As the rat surveyed the manger
Momentarily
Before proceeding to the wings
Where someone hit him,
Once, and then twice more,
With a heavy object,
Unmistakably, and in earnest.

MADONNAS TOUCHED UP WITH A GOATEE

Most ancient Metaphysics, (poor Metaphysics!)
All decked up in imitation jewelry.
We went for a stroll, arm in arm, smooching in public
Despite the difference in ages.

It's still the 19th century, she whispered.
We were in a knife-fighting neighborhood
Among some rundown relics of the Industrial Revolution.
Just a little further, she assured me,
In the back of a certain candy store only she knew about,
The customers were engrossed in the *Phenomenology of
    the Spirit*.

It's long past midnight, my dove, my angel!
We'd better be careful, I thought.
There were young hoods on street corners
With crosses and iron studs on their leather jackets.
They all looked like they'd read Darwin and that
    madman Pavlov,
And were about to ask us for a light.

FRONT TOOTH CROWNED WITH GOLD

Demonstrating the world's most amazing
Potato-peeler with a suitcase and a card table,
At the corner of two Pharaonic avenues,
Now badly rundown, boarded up, partly gutted;

In the galactic wind, in the hour
The cut-rate stores are already padlocked,
Their grilles lowered, only a few
Rat-faced old women still milling about . . .

And a hooker: scarlet wig, rabbit fur coat,
Hot pants, boots. Yes, she seems interested!
Inching closer, wide-eyed! Just for her
He's peeling his second, his third potato;

Himself in bad need of a shave:
Some Greek Arab Slav Scythian Longobard,
Gold tooth and no winter overcoat,
Everybody's venerable and future partner.

AUTUMN AIR

In ancient China,
I'm reminded,
They studied the feasibility
Of dispelling hunger
By eating air.

In some remote province,
Their lived a poor man
Who kept trying for years
To learn the difficult art.
Finally, one lean day
He summoned his sullen family.

His first steps were,
Reputedly,
Only slightly elevated,
But then he rose
Over the shacks, the outhouses —

High up there
Clutching his hat
Among the dragon-tailed,
Razor-studded kites,
On a day, let's say,
As blue as today.

III

DRAWING THE TRIANGLE

I reserve the triangle
For the wee hours,
The chigger-sized hours.

I like how it starts out
And never gets there.
I like how it starts out.

In the meantime, the bedroom window
Reflecting the owlish aspect
Of the face and the interior.

One hopes for tangents
Surreptitiously in attendance
Despite the rigors of the absolute.

INTERLUDE

A worm
In an otherwise
Red apple
Said: I am.

It happened on a chipped
China plate,
At a table
With twelve empty chairs.

The rightful owner
Of the apple
Had gone into the kitchen
To get a knife.

She was an old woman
Who forgot things easily.
Dear me,
She whispered.

JACKSTRAWS

The penny arcade silhouettes
Of a child and her mother
Frozen in gestures
Of sudden and exaggerated alarm.

Even a breath now
Might disturb what's left standing
On the mud-colored oilcloth
Nicked by nails, bread-knives,

In the circle of lamplight,
The maze of columns, fallen roof-beams,
Like a palace in ruins—
Perhaps the Chinese Emperor's?

The child with black bangs.
The woman with false eyelashes,
Who smokes too much,
Never goes to bed before 4 a.m.

MY WEARINESS OF EPIC PROPORTIONS

I like it when
Achilles
Gets killed
And even his buddy Patroclus—
And that hothead Hector—
And the whole Greek and Trojan
Jeunesse dorée
Is more or less
Expertly slaughtered
So there's finally
Peace and quiet
(The gods having momentarily
Shut up)
One can hear
A bird sing
And a daughter ask her mother
Whether she can go to the well
And of course she can
By that lovely little path
That winds through
The olive orchard

ANTEDILUVIAN CUSTOMS

We ate so well after the funeral
In that shack by the town dump;
Fingers dripping with barbecue sauce and grease
Making the quick sign of the cross
In the cramped, smoke-filled living room
Where they had a couple of card tables
Rigged up for the aunts and uncles and
    important neighbors;
The young widow sitting in the corner,
Her pillbox hat and black veil askew;
The three orphans urging us on with another bucket
Of that fierce homemade beer;
The cold spring night closing in.
                                        Eventually,
We had to kick the yellow bitch out
For fighting under the table with other quadrupeds.
We had to shut up Mr. Boisvert
Who forgot himself and started singing.
Still and all, it seemed foolish
To end the party right then and there.
What with you and me one foot in the grave!
The undertakers fortunately all invited.
The Reverend himself full of cheer,
Pinching the cook on the butt.
Ah, such a fine cook! Back in a minute
With young ducks roasted on spits,
And other soul-saving surprises!

GUARDIAN ANGEL

Grandmother often spoke of him
And his vigilance
On our behalf,
In these dark, hell-bent days.

She was sure he'd keep me
Out of harm's way.
She also confided,
I will get to see him sometime.

I forgot to ask her whether
I'd recognize him instantly,
Or whether he'd reveal himself to me
When the proper time came.

To this day I study
My neighbors closely.
I even peek nearsightedly
Into my shaving mirror.

ASTRAL MATTERS

Every so often someone climbs
To the top floor for a glimpse
Of the directors and their secretaries.

It's quiet and dusty up there
As if long after office hours.

With most of the bulbs out tonight,
Hard to make out the name and nature of
    each business
In the network of empty corridors
All painted midnight blue.

Still, how nice it would be
To catch a sight of a late-working executive
Of some Fire and Life Insurance Co.,
Turning a corner in a spiffy sharkskin suit.

Instead, there's the lavender-haired Venus
Limping on with mop and pail,

And beyond her, the usual
Three or four perpetual motion enthusiasts
Fogging the glass with their breath
Outside the dark patent office.

PUNCH MINUS JUDY

A row of mostly X-ed out windows.
One of them intact, open and darkly curtained,
Five stories up,
Where the elevated train slows down for a curve.

I glimpsed the world's skinniest arm
Coming between the slits, palm up,
To catch a drop of rain
At the sound of distant thunder.

Or another time, in a last bit of sultry daylight,
I saw two, cut-off at the elbows,
A small, naked babe
Raised in them, to breathe, briefly,

Above the boarded grocery store,
The three men drinking on the sidewalk,
The fourth one moving off, gimplegged,
Muttering to himself, I suppose.

DEAR ISAAC NEWTON

for Michael Cuddihy

Your famous apple
Is still falling.

Your red, ripe,
Properly notarized
Old Testament apple.

(The night's denseness is no help.)

All that we expostulated
To cause her to stay up there.

All the spells and curses
To hold and bind,
To enchant permanently
In the realm of seraphim.

She appeared to dilly dally, to consider.
She was already empyreal,
Ruled by some other reckoning,
When she shuddered and fell.

(The famous *malus pumila*.)

How heavy, how grave she grows
With each headlong instant
As though the seeds inside her
Were a catch of celestial razor-chips.

(Is she suffering for us, Isaac,
In some still incomprehensible way?)

Soon she'll rest at our feet.
Soon she'll strike the earth angrily,
For the earth's a pool table
The gravediggers have hewn with their spades.

Quickly then!
Make your bed,
Set your pillow on the apple
While she still spins.

Understand coldly
Impartially,
There's time only
For a single thought,

A single conjecture
As the bones rejoice in the earth,
As the maggots romp
In the Sunday roast . . .

(The famous apple up there.)

O she's falling lawfully,
But isn't she now
Perhaps even more mysterious
Than when she first started?

And wasn't that one of her
Prize worms
We saw crawling off
Into the unthinkable?

OLD MOUNTAIN ROAD

for Goody and Maida Smith

In the dusk of the evening
When the goats come,
Two pale ones nodding as they pass,
Unattended, taking their time
To graze by the curve,
Its sharpness indicated by a broken arrow,
In the last bit of daylight,

I saw a blonde little girl step
Out of nowhere, and bow to them, stiffly,
As one does at the conclusion of a school play,
And disappear, pinafore and all,
In the bushes, so that I sat
On my porch, dumbfounded . . .

The goats' intermittent tinkle
Growing fainter and fainter,
And then hushing, as if on cue,
For the whippoorwill to take over,
Briefly, in the giant maple.

Child! I thought of calling out,
Knowing myself a born doubter.

THE GREAT HORNED OWL

One morning the Grand Seigneur
Is so good as to appear.
He sits in a scrawny little tree
In my backyard.

When I say his name aloud,
He turns his head
And looks at me
In utter disbelief.

I show him my belt,
How I had to
Tighten it lately
To the final hole.

He ruffles his feathers,
Studies the empty woodshed,
The old red chevvy on blocks.
Alas! He's got to be going.

O MASTER

How come you're here
So damn early?

Nothing better to do
In the whole wide world
Than hang around my bed?

Couldn't even wait for me
To rub the crud out of my eyes?

Clear sky, sky so vast
And blue and you
Glum as the day you were born,
Standing there
With my leash and collar.

What you got for me today?

*

Had to get out of bed,
Look for nothing and no one,
And much else
That don't mean anything.

Clear sky
Long gone downwind.
Felt the chill
Up and down my spine.

Noticed I was barefooted,
The grass bristling
Between my pigeon-toes,

Witch grass.

DRAWN TO PERSPECTIVE

On a long block
Along which runs the wall
Of the House of Correction,
Someone has stopped
To holler the name
Of a son or a daughter.

Everything else in the world lies
As if in abeyance:
The warm summer evening;
The kid on roller skates;
The couple about to embrace
At the vanishing point.